Endorsements

Healing Is Possible is a beautiful invitation for all who are on a journey to reclaim wellness and balance within their mind, body and spirit. With a blend of storytelling, and accessible practices and spiritual teachings, this book is a sacred companion to anyone who is searching for healing. Sylvia generously offers her wisdom in ways that anyone can understand and implement in their lives. It's a beautiful offering to this world and one that I highly recommend.

Asha Frost
Indigenous Healer, Mentor, Ceremonial Speaker
Bestselling Author of *You are The Medicine*
www.ashafrost.com

If you have ever wondered how to navigate the sometimes-painful emotions you carry, look no further than this beautifully written book by Sylvia Plester-Silk. Drawing from her own experience as a survivor of abuse and trauma, and also as a Social Worker and energy healer, Sylvia gives very tangible and easy to do exercises designed to help you make peace with your past, release the trauma, manage emotions, set boundaries, discover who you are without the abuse, and reinvent yourself in a healthier and more whole version.

This book is short, but oh so powerful! Each chapter has activities that you can easily implement, and reading the healing journey that Sylvia went on will give you even more hope and inspiration.

I loved this book and know you will too!

Therese Skelly, M.A
The Intuitive Business Mentor
https://thereseskelly.com

Endorsements

Sylvia Plester-Silk has written a beautifully simple "go-to" book on healing. Not only does she teach us to honour our feelings, trust our intuition, and willingly enter the invisible realms for healing, but also helps us move into right relationship with ourselves. So much sacred feminine wisdom in these pages.

Andrea Menard
Performer, Speaker, and Author of *Seeds from the Sacred Feminine Wisdom Cards*
https://andreamenard.com

As an experienced therapist, Sylvia expertly uses her knowledge to help heal old wounds and encourage us all to move forward on a positive, fulfilling path. Sylvia's vulnerability emboldens the reader to implement her techniques that she masterfully describes through storytelling to help us all learn and grow.

Sami Jo Small
3x Olympian; 2x Olympic Gold Medallist
http://www.samijosmall.ca

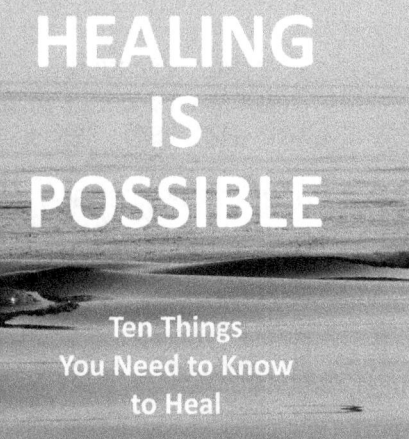

HEALING IS POSSIBLE:
Ten Things You Need to Know to Heal
Copyright © 2024 Sylvia Plester-Silk

ISBN: 978-1-990330-66-7

All rights reserved. No portion of this book may be reproduced mechanically, electronically, or by any other means, including photocopying, without permission of the author except in the case of brief quotations embodied in critical articles and reviews. It is illegal to copy this book, post it to a website, or distribute it by any other means without permission from the author.

Limits of Liability and Disclaimer of Warranty
The author and publisher shall not be liable for your misuse of the enclosed material. This book is strictly for informational and educational purposes only.

Publisher
One Thousand Trees
www.onethousandtrees.com

"The healing is the learning, understanding, acceptance and caring for yourself, so that once you have done that in its completeness, you can share that illumination outside of yourself. It is very important that you put this into practice now, having deep compassion, giving yourself deep permission, and accepting that, in this moment, in every moment of every day. You are full and complete and beautiful. Even when you think you are messed up, the biggest mess-up that could possibly happen in that time, there is beauty and excellence in it. Stand back, see the reflection of yourself in others, and of others in yourself, and know there is no brokenness. There is only growth here."

Akashic Teaching September 24, 2020

Contents

Acknowledgements xi
Introduction: Healing is Possible xiii

Chapter 1: Everything is Energy 1
Chapter 2: Feelings Are Fluid 9
Chapter 3: You Are Not What Happened to You 17
Chapter 4: Patterns Are Created 25
Chapter 5: Anxiety is a Mind Sport 35
Chapter 6: Master Patterns Process 43
Chapter 7: Empaths 51
Chapter 8: Intuition 63
Chapter 9: Recognizing Your Strengths 71
Chapter 10: Forgiveness and Letting Go 77

Kind People 85
About the Author 89

Acknowledgements

Thank you to my husband, who has always had my back in life. I love you, Mark.

I want to thank my clients. Your willingness to be open and vulnerable and to allow me to witness your healing has been an incredible gift in my life. You have taught me so much!

I am grateful to my teachers along the way. Whether it was through challenge or support, I appreciate your role in my healing, work, and life.

So many of you have walked beside me on my journey. To my people: the therapists, healers, course teachers, friends along my path, and business coaches. Thank you for all you shared with me and for believing in me when I was shaky about my capabilities. Many of you held me up when I felt weak and reflected my true self back to me. I now see It. I believe in me!

My dog Josee came into my life and challenged me to believe in myself fully.

My editor, Lisa, helped me find the path to one book from a rough idea. She created the timeline I so much needed to shift this from idea to completion – supporting me along the path! I am grateful!

Introduction

Healing is Possible

When I reflect back over my life, I realize that I have deeply changed. I have gone from being a shy, fearful child to a bold, confident, assertive adult.

Some of my lessons were gently learned. Many were not.

It seems the most powerful gifts of learning didn't feel like gifts at the time, and involved a great deal of hurt, sadness, and even anger. I know that I could have stayed in these emotions and become a victim of circumstance, yet part of me deeply yearned for a better, more loving experience of life.

My healing journey started quite early in life. I believe it was highly influenced by my choice of careers. Having the opportunity to see a career coach when I was

18 years old, I had my first experience with a psychologist. She had me list my interests, skills, and what I was good at. Then she sent me off to Ryerson Polytechnical Institute (now Toronto Metropolitan University) to do some research. I discovered that Social Work was a thing. Coming from a very small town, I didn't know of this profession. That fall, I was enrolled in Ryerson's Social Work program.

I learned the power of therapy while attending and watching people grow. I learned that I could make changes that better suited me and my life, and that it was okay to seek support when things were difficult in life.

I find myself making jokes about my family being functional and healthy until I graduated with my Bachelor of Social Work degree, and once I graduated, they got messed up. The truth was that I had another experience and learned about healthy emotions, communications, and about abuse.

Within a few years, my father had a heart attack. I went into crisis. I had not dealt with how his sexually inappropriate behaviour, along with some physical violent behaviour, impacted me. Subconsciously, I was frightened that he would die before I got any sense of resolution to my trauma. I started the search for a therapist. It was not easy.

    I started with an elderly woman about the age of my father, and there was no way that I could share my story with her. The thought, at 23 years old, of sharing sexual abuse with her was humiliating. She discharged me from her care at the second session, as she felt my needs were too great for her ability to meet them. I felt rejected, and knew I wanted to feel better, so I continued my search. I started with a social worker who was easier to talk with, and who was so great at her job that she got a promotion, and my care had to be transferred again.

    They say, three times lucky, and this was the case. I was transferred to Trish, who was much younger and literally changed my life! I experienced unconditional love and caring for the first time in my life. I knew I could tell her my fears, my mistakes, and all about my abuse. She was my rock! I can't say enough about my gratitude to her – she helped me learn how to feel my emotions and name them. My feeling vocabulary went from fear or guilty to a rainbow of emotions. Through her gentle care, I was able to realize that I wasn't broken, that I was valuable. That I truly mattered.

For me, it was the beginning of a long, very rewarding journey in self-discovery and personal growth.

I now feel a sense of personal happiness, freedom, and purpose that I wish for all my readers. I invite you to sit back, read and reflect on your life with self-compassion and growth in mind. You too can heal.

Chapter 1

Everything is Energy

In 1995, I facilitated a talk therapy group for family members of addicted people. My group was co-facilitated by a volunteer who recently learned what to me was a strange Therapeutic Touch technique. I had never heard of such a strange idea—that you could move your hands around someone's "energy field" (whatever that was) and help them heal from physical pain.

One evening, I had a headache and mentioned it to her. She excitedly offered me a Therapeutic Touch treatment. I may have rolled my eyes, thinking this was a lot of malarky. How could such a far-out concept have any basis in reality? What was this "energy" thing anyway? She was so excited to provide it that I decided to appease her and say yes. I was sure she would feel like she had done something to help me, and I was confident she would not hurt me.

Within a minute or so of her starting my treatment, my headache flew off the top of my head like a bad toupee on a windy day. All the ache was gone. I was shocked and in disbelief!

Over the next few days, my disbelief shifted to curiosity. How could this have happened? I needed to know more.

Within two weeks of that first Therapeutic Touch experience, I was attending my Level One Therapeutic Touch class, and my life has never been the same since.

We started by learning about the energy field that surrounds our physical bodies. Once we were taught it, we got to experience it. We started by holding our hands, palms facing one another, a few feet apart and then bringing them together. I felt a warm, tingling sensation—it was odd. My curiosity grew.

Next, we had to sense another person's energy. I was terrified of failing this exercise, so I decided to go through the motions and see what happened. Taking a deep breath, I felt my partner's energy different from my own—it was heavier and a bit grey. I was intrigued. I thought there was no way I could feel another's energy, but I was surprised that this was possible for me!

How to Sense Energy:

Hold your hands out in front of you, palms facing each other about 3 feet apart. Allow your fingers to curve slightly, forming a cup with your hands. You might like to close your eyes or find a spot to focus on. Now, very slowly bring your palms together as you place your awareness on the space between them. As you get closer, you may experience a sensation.

Feeling another's energy in this way may feel like pushing or pulling; others may feel tingling or a sense of warmth or cool. What do you experience?

Now, try this practice with another person. Make sure you are grounded (see page 5). Stand or sit facing one another. One person holds their palms facing up and the other places their hands palms down approximately 18 inches above their partner's hands. Very slowly, move the upper hands towards the lower. What do you sense as your palms slowly come closer? How is it similar to and different from what you feel, sense or experience with your own energy?

You are feeling energy. Cool, eh?

Our aura surrounds our human body and can reach several feet from our physical body. When you did the palm-to-palm exercise, you sensed your aura and another person's aura.

Like a fax machine, energy can be transmitted from one person to another. We can sense and feel energy from others. Have you ever randomly thought of someone, then phoned or texted them, and they were struggling with something and needed your support? You felt their energy remotely and responded.

Other people's energy influences us. Think about a time you had to go to a social event but didn't feel like it. Given the importance of the occasion, you decided you should go and did so, only to find that within a few minutes of arriving, you were suddenly having fun, feeling energized, and in a better mood. This is the impact of other people's energy on you. You got caught up in the party's vibe or the energy of others' auras.

I remember a time when I was going to Ryerson in the 1980's. It was a Friday afternoon, a rare weekend with no essays to write, nor tests to study for. Smiling, feeling relaxed, I slowly walked to the subway, feeling I had all the time in the world. As I entered the subway, I noticed myself starting to rush. Before I knew it, I was running towards the incoming train door. I had been swept up in the rush hour energy of those around me. It can be a powerful influence in our lives.

Because another person's energy can impact us, we must learn to ground ourselves.

How do you feel when you are in nature? Around big trees, a large body of water, or near a meadow? I feel very relaxed. If I have been stressed, I will often sigh. As I meld with the energy or aura of the forest or lake, I find myself feeling calm, relaxed, and refreshed.

How to Ground Yourself:

- Sit comfortably in a chair with your feet flat on the floor. Notice your breathing in the moment.

- Straighten your spine as much as is comfortable for you.

- Now, bring your attention to the soles of your feet.

- Imagine roots growing out of the balls of your feet down through the floor deep, deep into the earth's surface to the core of the earth. Trust whatever type of roots you see or imagine are perfect for you.

- You now notice a giant boulder in the centre of the earth and allow those roots to grow around the boulder.

Notice how you feel. How is your breathing? How are you feeling in your body?

Clients often describe themselves as breathing more deeply, their feet feeling heavy, and being more relaxed.

Energy can shift. As I mentioned at the beginning of this chapter, when someone with skills tunes into your energy from a place of loving compassion, they can assist you in relaxing, and letting go of emotional and physical discomfort and pain.

You can heal from your traumas. Learn to feel those feelings and release them.

These are skills anyone can learn. I will share some releasing techniques in later chapters of the book.

Chapter 2

Feelings Are Fluid

Emotions are meant to be fluid. We feel them, they shift, and we go on with our day.

Most clients come to me with a long history of avoiding their emotions. As a coping strategy, avoiding uncomfortable emotions works until one day when it is no longer effective. When we repress emotions of hurt, fear and anger, we cannot experience complete happiness, joy and emotional freedom.

Think of a pressure cooker; it needs to release steam to function safely. Feelings are similar; when we hide our emotions and negate them, we run the risk of them exploding. This often happens at the most inconvenient of times and can lead to embarrassment. On the other hand, as we learn to feel our emotions, we 'let the pressure off' and we feel calmer, more in control, and happier.

As we ignore our emotions, they become locked into our cells and will eventually escape in some way. Many people experience increased stress, anxiety, depression, or physical illness when this happens. Others find themselves with angry outbursts or becoming easily overwhelmed by life events. These behaviours negatively affect our relationships, friendships, and careers.

We are often taught not to feel in childhood. Sometimes by well-meaning adults in our lives, or by peers who tease us when we are vulnerable. We get messages and create rules to live our lives by.

The childhood messages I received were, "You are too sensitive" and "Stop your crying, or I'll give you something to cry about." The underlying message was to stop feeling. I began to believe that something was wrong with me, that I was flawed. I tried to hide my emotions. Then I would cry when I was angry and feel that I had betrayed myself by being vulnerable with others when I didn't want to be.

What messages did you receive? How do these play out in your life?

We are often told not to cry, not to get upset, and that anger is unhealthy. People talk about negative emotions and positive emotions. Feelings get a bad rap, yet they are our body's way of telling us that we are alive and responding to our current situation. I don't believe in negative emotions. All emotions are positive if we feel them and let them go.

The cool thing is that humans have access to a multitude of emotions. All are healthy when acknowledged, felt, and then released. A few months back, I told a client that emotions are meant to be fluid. We feel them, they shift, and we go on with our day.

However, when we experience a trauma response, emotion becomes locked into our cells. It becomes a permanent state of being, one that is possible to unfreeze.

Many fear that when they begin to experience their emotions, they won't be able to shut them down. If this is you, let me remind you how incredibly skilled you are at not feeling. You are more likely to shut them down than be completely out of control. As I have recommended to clients, set a timer at first for 5 minutes, then allow yourself time to feel, cry, and just be present with where you are at in the moment. When the timer goes off, get up and carry on with your day.

When I went into therapy in my 20's, the only emotions I was aware of were guilt and fear. I was very limited in my ability to acknowledge my emotions. My therapist encouraged me to keep naming my feelings until I became friends with them. It was like learning a brand-new language.

Throughout my career, I have discovered that most emotions are experienced as physical sensations in the torso. For example, children will talk about having butterflies in their tummies. They are often feeling excitement or nervousness.

Let me share the process I use to teach my clients to become emotionally literate.

How to Become Friends with Your Emotions:

Scan your torso in your mind's eye. Take time to notice any physical sensations, and name them. For example, you may feel a tightness in your chest or a void in your stomach. Name it as a physical sensation.

Now, focus on the emojis on page 15. Notice the names of the feeling, below each emoji. As you focus on your physical sensation, try on each feeling and emoji to see if it resonates with the physical sensation. If not, go to the next emotion until you sense a slight shift in the physical sensation. This shift feels like sharing something with another person and feeling heard. It's like an internal sense of validating yourself.

Then, name the emotion(s) you are feeling.

Write down the sensations and the emotions. You will start to create your own personal dictionary of your feelings.

Repeat this practice several times a day. For some folks, it takes a week, and for others, it can take over a month to really get to know their emotions.

Trust me, when you start this process, you will find that your feelings are more manageable. You will also notice that they are fluid, and change throughout your day. And remember to celebrate your success in getting to know yourself better.

In this way, you can process your emotions as they arise today, and it becomes easier to feel the painful emotions linked to your past and/or your trauma. You will be able to share more openly with those around you, and better contain and manage even the most challenging emotions.

Helpful Hint: Journalling your feelings and the circumstances can be really helpful in this process. Allowing yourself to have a special book that you use only for this purpose is helpful. Use the stream-of-consciousness technique; just begin to write. Don't worry about neatness, grammar, spelling, or if it even makes sense. Simply allow yourself to be present with what you are experiencing in the moment. This will allow you to better understand some of the underlying beliefs that you have. We will address how to shift beliefs in another chapter.

Today, I feel...

Anxious	Bashful	Cheerful	Confused	Content	Disappointed
Disgusted	Distressed	Embarrassed	Enraged	Excited	Fear
Frustrated	Furious	Grateful	Grief	Guilty	Hopeless
Hurt	Intimidated	Irritated	Lonely	Lost	Nervous
Pleased	Regret	Relaxed	Remorse	Satisfied	Shocked
Terrified	Thrilled	Trapped	Uncomfortable	Upset	Worthless

© 2021 Sylvia Plester-Silk, RSW

On Purpose TRANSFORMATIONS

Chapter 3

You Are Not What Happened to You

Women often identify as a role, such as a wife, mother, daughter, social worker, etc. We take on roles as identities, meaning that we use them to define who we are.

This also extends to things that happen to us.

How many of us identify as a victim of abuse or a survivor of abuse?

When we take on these identities, we limit our vision of ourselves to what happened to us.

Take these two sentences, for example:

1. I am a survivor of abuse.
2. I survived abuse.

Can you see in the second statement that it identifies an experience and is not owned as a permanent identity?

My abuse does not define me, and I am more clearly defined by how I live my life.

When we use the *I am* statement, we allow another's behaviour to define who we are.

For years, I identified as a survivor of abuse. I allowed it to define and limit me. Once I was able to heal from the impact of the abuse, I realized what I was doing. You see, I was giving my father's behaviour permanent control over how I defined myself.

I decided to take my power back.

Yes, I had experiences of sexual abuse. Yes, I had experiences of physical abuse. Yes, I had experiences of emotional abuse. Yet, this is not who I am. I no longer will be defined by it.

I am a vibrant, loving, capable person. I have healed from believing that I am broken or flawed because of my past experiences. (Hint: you are not either.)

I have put the responsibility back onto my abusers. They were adults and chose to act in the ways they did. I did not invite it. I did not deserve it.

Nor did you!

From an energetic lens, the people we interact with influence our energy fields. From a stranger who smiles at you as you walk by to those who are grumpy with you, everyone impacts your energy in some way (more on this in the Empaths chapter).

Just imagine how we can be holding the energy of the abuser in our bodies and fields, and it is impacting us on a daily basis. We talk about somatic experiencing—that we hold the memories of past events in our physical bodies.

When we are abused, the energy of the abuser is transferred to us. When someone is being abusive, they tend to blame their victim because if they took responsibility, it would be difficult to continue their behaviour. Often, a lot of anger, self-loathing, and blaming energy is transferred to the individual being abused. Then, this energy transfer can cause confusion because we subconsciously accept the blame energy and then shift into faulty beliefs about ourselves. We are not even aware of it.

The good news is that we can release that energy that is not ours from our bodies. We do that when we feel the emotions related to the abuse and share them with a safe person.

We deserve to be free of the abuser's energy to find parts of ourselves again. Following is an energy-based technique to help you intentionally release their energy.

Make sure that you have time to do this exercise, and lots of time afterwards to process this (it's a deeper process than it appears).

- Make sure you are grounded and in a safe place for you.

- Allow your awareness to go to your body and sense where your abuser's energy is on you. Just simply acknowledge it.

- Keep breathing.

- Now state assertively, "I now return this energy to (Insert abuser's name here)."

- Take a deep breath.

- Allow that energy to flow out of your body and energy field into that person's higher, all-knowing self.

- Now, imagine you are standing in the most beautiful waterfall. The water is flowing at the perfect speed for you, and the water temperature is lovely. Allow this water energy to flow in and around your body, filling up the voids with divine energy.

- Now get up, move, and experience how this feels in your body.

Now that you have released the abuser's energy, it's time to reflect on your personal power and acknowledge what you have learned and gained as a result of your challenging experiences.

One thing that helped me was realizing what I gained because of how I was brought up. For example, I am very independent, can figure things out independently, and am incredibly creative when resources are limited. This is who I am. Not my abuse.

I asked a client what she gained from how her father treated her. She was shocked by the question and then realized that she had qualities that her abuser couldn't and didn't take away from her. That is her true identity. Not the abuse.

It was powerful for her to recognize that her very essence as a human being was still intact despite years of daily emotional abuse. She is very creative and very loving, among many other skills.

Take out your journal and answer these questions:

- When you experienced the abuse, what behaviours did you discover that helped you to get through it at the time?

- What special skills do others tell you that you are good at? Look for repetitive feedback that you have received. Write it all down.

- What comes so easily to you that you are shocked when others can't do it? These are often the hidden strengths that you have devalued because they come so easy to you that you might think—doesn't everyone know how to do it?

- What abilities are you most proud of? (It's okay to write them down; you are not being too full of yourself!)

You now have a list of your abilities and aspects of yourself that are valuable to you.

Take time to celebrate your abilities and who you really are! Do something in way of celebration, such as dance, grab your favourite coffee or tea, or if your budget allows, you might purchase a memento that reminds you of your inner strengths and abilities!

You are not your abuse. You are so much more!

You are a beautiful, skilled, talented being. As you peel back the layers, please celebrate yourself on a daily basis.

Allow your inner light to glow as you honour your true self!

Chapter 4

Patterns Are Created

In a moment, we create a pattern. It is not a conscious choice, per se, but an unconscious process that gets locked in our cells, bodies, and unconscious memories. These patterns are established in a fleeting moment.

Patterns are an interlocking of feelings, thoughts, and beliefs. When one of these aspects of patterns comes into our awareness, our body has a physical response.

Once a pattern is developed, it quickly becomes part of your personal operating manual of behaviour. When another situation arises that is remotely similar to the original situation, your subconscious will provide that pattern as a solution, whether it is appropriate to the current event or not.

It is a truly brilliant solution! And it's created in a matter of seconds, with the best intentions to support and assist you.

When we have previous patterns in our operating manual, we build new patterns based on them. One pattern may be truly remarkable, powerful, and make sense. Yet, the subsequent patterns will fit the path of the previously created pattern, which is already part of our operating system and may be illogical.

When a pattern is created due to a trauma, it will almost always have a self-critical belief in it, coupled with the emotional response to the abusive, or traumatic event that we don't process at the time.

For example, you get laid off from a job that you excelled at, as part of downsizing. In the moment, you experience fear. You think to yourself, "I will never get another job." Under the surface, the pattern playing out might be: At the age of 8 when you didn't get the part in the play at school you really wanted, you decided that you weren't talented enough or skilled enough, and you decided to give up acting. Your response in the present moment might be: You find yourself lamenting around your home, self-criticizing your skill set, distracting yourself from working on your resumé or even looking at career opportunities that excite you. You know you need to get another job, but just can't take action. Can you see how your response can be controlled by a previous pattern?

When a similar circumstance triggers the past pattern, the pattern will arise to protect you time and time again. It is a way for you not to experience pain, even if it is not what you truly need nor desire in the moment. And it may not fit your current circumstance. Secretly you may wonder why you are acting this way, wondering what your problem is and then beating yourself up for it.

These patterns are created moment by moment. Often resulting from a minute circumstance, your mind creates a story about you and forevermore acts as if this is true. For example, if you are feeling powerless, your subconscious might decide that the only way to survive (or have power) is to people-please, try to be invisible, or fight back, and so on. Each person will develop their patterns based on personal experience, family dynamics, friendships and other life events.

These are often called faulty beliefs. They are beliefs based on an emotional injury, a sense of powerlessness in a single moment in time. For example, the thoughts might be, "I am only safe when others are happy with me." "I am only safe when no one notices me." "I have to fight for myself because no one will protect me."

The pattern consists of a thought or belief and an emotion, and is often experienced with a physical response. For example, you may feel a pulling sensation in your chest when others important to you are unhappy. You may experience a feeling of shrinking if you are the centre of attention. Another person may experience a burning sensation when they sense the need to protect themselves. Each person's physical response may differ from situation to situation.

This pattern becomes locked into your subconscious, and your reactions to a potential situation often happen without your awareness. You may find yourself compulsively helping others at your own expense.

This is what happens when we have a specific goal we desire, and time and time again, we sabotage our best intentions.

Here's an example of how a pattern can play out.

At age 13, when I told my mother about my father's sexual abuse, she said, "That's how he shows his love for you." I told her to tell him to stop loving me. I didn't want the abuse. Nothing changed as a result of speaking up.

My lesson: If you weren't treating me right, speaking up about it didn't work, so it was best to walk away quietly with as little reaction as possible. This became a deeply entrenched pattern for me.

I used this many times when I should have spoken up for myself. Instead of any sort of conflict, I would stop calling the other person and fade into the sunset. I had learned young to cope alone because I could trust and rely on myself. Others, not so much.

When we remain unconscious of our patterns, they run us. We make choices at the moment that do not serve us well.

Many therapies work on conscious awareness as the solution. Cognitive Behaviour Therapy encourages people to become aware of the components of the pattern and ask if the beliefs are accurate. Behaviour therapy seeks to shift the behaviour just before the undesired behaviour and outcome occur.

Yet, with this awareness, we often get frustrated with ourselves. How often have you heard someone say they wanted to stop a behaviour and yet have relapsed into the undesired outcome? Many people come to see me with awareness of the behaviour pattern but not the underlying pattern operating in their lives. Nor the recognition of why they did what they did. I have been told by many clients, "I don't know why I relapsed. I thought my life was going great, and before I knew it, I was drinking/shopping/gambling/having another affair, etc."

These patterns are the basis of life challenges such as addiction, self-harm, and self-sabotage.

Awareness on its own is great. It allows us to have the option or the sense that we are have a choice. We need to go even deeper than the awareness of the pattern to the root cause of its creation. Hint: it is often in childhood.

Sometimes patterns can be intertwined with other patterns, and they become even more confusing. You may need to release one aspect or pattern, and will find that another one shows up. At times, we clear an aspect and experience the freedom, only months or years later to discover there is another pattern related. It's not that the first pattern wasn't released; it is just the intertwined nature of these unconscious patterns. We do the work, and then we know we can do even deeper work.

This is challenging to do for ourselves, and often requires a skilled, non-judgmental witness to listen and distill the underlying patterns and then release them.

I do this daily for my clients using intuition and a pendulum. I have repeatedly witnessed people shifting patterns and quickly developing new, healthy patterns, which emerge spontaneously once the outdated one is released. These patterns tend to have more choice and personal power in them.

Here's some exercises to help you.

Think of one of your patterns that you would like to shift.

In your imagination, take yourself back to the moment before you engaged in the undesired behaviour. What emotion were you experiencing?

What were you thinking about yourself?

How old did you feel? This often indicates the age you developed the original pattern. It can help identify the situation that you created the unconscious pattern in response to.

At the age you identified, what happened that is any way related to the current emotions and thoughts you have? This may not seem related, but just allow yourself to have the situation come into your awareness.

Can you bring some compassion to that younger self?

Imagine responding to that younger self part with loving compassion from your current self. Can you comfort that part, acknowledging that its role is here to help, but that it lacks the ability to release without feeling the original emotions? Can you understand that the thought is based on a moment in time and may not be accurate? Can you see yourself hugging your younger part and offering reassurance? Once you have really attended to this younger part, can you ask its permission to release the pattern?

Note: Chapter 6 includes some information about the Master Patterns Process, which can help you to release the remainder of this earlier pattern.

If there is an emotional charge to the current situation, run it through the Master Patterns Process as well.

Still stuck? Then reach out for help to a trusted person who knows how to release the energy related to these situations. Remember, the intertwined patterns can be tricky to release, or it may take several attempts to release all the patterns underlying a behaviour.

Be gentle with yourself. You are making progress, and you can heal.

Chapter 5

Anxiety is a Mind Sport

Anxiety is a symptom that you are experiencing an emotion with which you are out of touch. In other words, you have an unmet need that is trying to get your attention.

Anxiety is never real, nor in real-time.

Think about it: when you feel anxious, your thoughts race a mile a minute about what bad outcome might happen. It's always a future-focused process. Yes, your heart races, and you might have difficulty breathing in the moment, but your thoughts that evoke stress are all in the future. And most of the thoughts are not based on your reality.

Many people grew up in homes that felt unsafe. They experienced trauma and were not supported in their feelings. When you have a lot of suppressed emotion, you are more at risk of experiencing anxiety. As a child, you may have spent so much time anticipating negative events that being future-focused was a key survival skill.

For healing to happen, it is very important that you learn to identify and respond to your emotions. This can be challenging when, as a child, you witness emotions being ignored or are given direct messages that your emotions are not welcome or important.

When you are experiencing anxiety, you are not living in the present moment. Your mind has taken over and is in the driver's seat. You need to take your mind and put it in the passenger seat because it's spouting off thoughts that are not accurate at the moment—and it can't be trusted to drive. Many of these thoughts have no basis in your current reality.

Years ago, I burned out from stress in my job. I became depressed, and experienced anxiety as part of my depression. When I went off sick, I barely spoke for 3 days because forming words took more effort than I could muster. I was emotionally and physically exhausted. A few weeks later, my husband, who is colour-blind, decided to paint his truck. He asked me to help him choose a colour at the paint store. I felt uncomfortable leaving the house for fear that someone at work would see me out and think I was faking my depression. (You do hear the distorted thinking here, right?) Feeling insecure and frightened, I challenged myself and went to the store with him. I was in the store for about two minutes when anxiety set in. I began to panic, feeling I couldn't breathe; I wasn't safe, I was going to be found out! I grabbed a paint swatch and fled out the door at high speed. I ran to the truck, climbed in and locked the door. My rapid breathing didn't subside until I was back in my house. Fortunately, I was in therapy and receiving regular Therapeutic Touch treatments, so I was able to work through this anxiety to understand why I acted in such a strange way. It was almost a full-on anxiety attack. I am grateful I have never experienced this before or since this event. But nothing my mind told me in this scenario was accurate. I had only been off work with severe depression for 2 weeks! I wasn't faking it! I was genuinely depressed and working on recovering from it. My recovery was dependent on going out and doing things to build up my coping skills and to get better.

In this scenario, I wasn't living in the moment but in my head. My mind had taken me hostage. It lied to me and made me feel threatened because it saw any co-workers as a threat to me and my job. This is what the mind does. It is not your friend—it is a critical, judgmental bully. It will talk you out of listening to your feelings, your body wisdom, and your intuition.

Sometimes, the mind will take tiny pieces of evidence based on past experiences and create stories that magnify these "facts" to such an exaggerated extent that they are terrifying. Or it will play on fears and amplify them to an unrealistic extent.

Then, we feel anxiety. The mind goes to town, rapidly firing off fear and anxiety-inducing thoughts. Our bodies respond as if those thoughts are accurate. Yet, they're not.

Part of healing is learning to honour yourself fully. Listening and responding to your current emotions is a powerful healing technique. The weird thing is that we spend so much time avoiding emotion, but when we learn to feel, witness, and honour it, the feelings will release on their own.

The more you give in to anxiety, the more it grows and controls you. Perhaps it starts when you avoid one uncomfortable situation based on anxious thoughts. Then, your mind incipiently creates thoughts that many things are unsafe. The more you listen, the more power you give the critical mind, empowering it, not you! And slowly, your world shrinks, one decision at a time. Over time, some people can no longer drive their cars or leave their homes.

So, I invite you to push back on your anxiety! Expand your world!

To overcome anxiety, you need to learn to enter the present moment, to shift from mind awareness to body awareness.

Here's what I teach my clients to become present in the moment when they are experiencing anxiety:

- Breathe.

- Ground yourself as described in Chapter 1.

- Use the Identify Your Emotions exercise from Chapter 2.

- Hint: it's not only anxiety; what else is happening in your torso now?

- What is below the racing heart or difficulty breathing?

- Take a deep breath and scan your torso for a moment.

- What are the needs you have that the emotion is asking for?

Feelings are our body's way of letting us know we are alive and having an experience. They often create awareness of a need. For example, you may need comfort or a non-judgmental listening ear if you are sad.

- If you are angry, you may need to shift your behaviour or have a conversation.

- If you are hungry, have something to eat.

- If you are afraid, you may need reassurance.

Respond in a healthy way by acknowledging and feeling the emotion. Next, respond according to your identified need at the current moment, and take action to fulfill that need.

Write your experience in your journal so that you have a different experience that you can revisit when you experience anxious thoughts again.

This is only one method of becoming present in the moment. You might also like to try mindfulness practices and meditation. Meditation can involve walking in nature, engaging in a craft, or walking through the trees or near the water.

You deserve the freedom that comes from living in the moment—that moment when the mind quiets itself, and you simply breathe. You will find yourself calmer, and breathing will be easier.

Chapter 6

Master Patterns Process

As you will remember from Chapter 4, patterns can be complex to release when we only focus on conscious awareness. Many of these patterns link back to childhood when an event happened that we created a story about in our unconscious. Many of these stories are based on our limited understanding of our world at the time. These stories then map our behaviour as we accept them as our truth.

So, imagine how incredibly freeing it can be to learn how to depattern these, bring the unconscious into our awareness, and have the opportunity to live differently from a place of choice vs. reaction that is pre-programmed from an old, outdated belief. This is where the true power of choice resides for all of us.

In 2016, I participated in a year-long depatterning program that worked with specific thoughts of each pattern, sometimes doing multiple clearings for one pattern over several days. It was incredible and life-changing for me. I still use the process daily.

Those who know me well know that I'm an impatient person. If there is a way to make things easier or more efficient, I will find it and do it. This is why the vast majority of my client work is facilitated by energy work – it's faster, gentler, and less work for clients and for me. It is more effective than verbally processing past events or focusing on thoughts and behaviour alone.

During the program, I began to wonder how one might be able to re-pattern an entire pattern instead of layer by layer, as this process I was learning did.

I started journalling about it, using an intuitive journalling process to create the Releasing Master Patterns Technique.

By master patterns, I mean patterns we repetitively play out behaviourally in our lives. The ones where we might say to ourselves, "Why did I do that again – I promised I would change that outcome," or we hear feedback from a few others we trust that have our best interests in mind, "You often do …. (insert behaviour here.)" It helps release these patterns that make no sense to us – to unlock new behaviours and free us up for novel experiences. It invites more joy into our lives.

One key aspect of this work is being very honest and self-reflective with yourself. Make sure you are kind and compassionate to yourself as you do this work. It can be easy to criticize yourself. Remember, patterns are created unconsciously.

You may need to journal and ask yourself deeper questions to get to the crux of each area of the pattern, such as feelings, actions, thoughts, etc.

Journalling as a Tool for Understanding:

Journalling with the stream-of-consciousness technique is powerful. I recommend getting a book and pen, as you have more access to your unconscious when you write than when you type into a computer.

Start the journalling process with what you are consciously aware of, then allow your pen to write without concern for spelling, grammar, or neatness. Sometimes, a change in handwriting becomes a signal of something vital for you to notice. Recently, when I was triggered, I journalled about it, and the inner child part of me wrote in tiny little writing that was so light on the pen that it was difficult to read. My regular handwriting is quite large, and this stands out. When I re-read the journal entry, this difference in writing and what I accessed in my unconscious was a powerful message to be depatterned.

Back to the Master Patterns Technique: I tested this process with a women's group of about 50 people. Many of them found it helpful, relaxing and freeing.

One individual approached me a few months after the event to share how freeing it was for her. She had been let go from a position in a company she had held for several years. She had been devastated and partly angry with one of the women involved in her dismissal, which still impacted her a few years after the original event. She had difficulty sleeping, eating, and in the business she had started. Once she had completed the Master Patterns Technique, she found that with the release of all the feelings of angst, her behaviour shifted, and she felt free and slept much better. My wish is that it has the same benefit for you!

This is what I created.

Releasing Master Patterns Technique

Create conscious awareness of all aspects of the pattern. It will be vital to take notes for this, as you will forget part of it. You may wish to review your journal to get some of these repetitive aspects of the pattern from which you want to be released.

Feelings—You will want to narrow it down to the 1 or 2 deeper emotions that you experience when you think of the upsetting situation.

Actions—What actions or behaviours do you engage in when this pattern arises?

Thoughts—What do you think about yourself? About others? About people in general? The idea here is to listen to your inner dialogue and get to the core of the pattern.

Beliefs—Bear witness to the beliefs about yourself and life that come up. They may even be contradictive to your thoughts. (Remember, patterns often don't make sense!)

Impact of these—when you have these feelings, thoughts and beliefs, what tends to result when the pattern is acted out?

Questions to ask when journalling to get really clear on how the pattern impacts your life:

- How do the parts of the pattern show up in your thoughts and your behaviour?

- Each time the patterns show up, how do you feel?

- What behaviour(s) and outcome(s) do you experience when the pattern is present?

- How do you act?

- What results do you hope for each time you engage in this pattern?

Reflecting on your answers to the above, can you see the incongruence between your goals or desires for the pattern vs. the actual reality of what occurs in your life?

Do you have any resistance to releasing this? If yes, notice where it is located in your body. Acknowledge it. Don't try to change it; instead, just be aware of it.

Do you have any judgments about yourself in this pattern?

Imagine removing the energy of any resistance and judgment like an old rag. See yourself removing the rag with these energies attached, and allow the cloth to go to the universe, god, or divine.

Next, hold the pattern in conscious awareness without judgment. Be willing to let go of the pattern with the intention of receiving something more or better.

Now fill in the blanks of the following statement:

When I feel (Insert your emotion(s) here) and I (do, act) (name the behaviour(s) I get (insert results). This is not working for me. I release it and let it go.

Now say the above statement assertively and take a deep breath.

See the statement written inside a bubble. Notice that that bubble is now separate from you and your body. See that bubble float up into the sky until you can no longer see it.

Get up and go about your day.

When I have used this process, it has been quite powerful. We are inviting ourselves to release that which no longer serves us in order to create space for another pattern that will be more life-enhancing for us!

I invite you to try it out. The first time you do this, start with a simple pattern and then build up to more challenging patterns. You can do this.

Chapter 7

Empaths

Are you an empath? If you're not sure, complete the questionnaire on pages 52-53.

We have all heard how incredibly powerful having empathy can be. It is a trait of very successful leaders and therapists, among others who have Emotional Intelligence. It helps us care for one another and appreciate the experience of others.

When we talk about empaths, they tend to be labelled as overly sensitive and in need of thicker skin by non-empaths who wonder what their problem is.

Empaths are those sensitive folks with a deep compassion for others. So much caring for others that they tend to take on the symptoms of others. It is a powerful gift when we learn how to manage it effectively.

Healing is Possible

Sylvia Plester-Silk, RSW
sylvia@OnPurposeTransformations.ca
www.OnPurposeTransformations.ca
519.822.3776

Empaths Self-Assessment:

Please rate each question on the following scale:

1	2	3	4	5
I don't relate		Sometimes		Totally Me!

1.	I have been told I was too sensitive or too emotional as a child.	
2.	Being around people who are fighting, yelling, or arguing causes me distress.	
3.	I find being in crowds tiring and often need to have quiet time to regenerate afterwards.	
4.	I easily feel overwhelmed by sensory stimuli such as loud noises, non-stop talkers, or odors.	
5.	I often feel drained, or agitated when leaving crowded places like the mall, outdoor venues.	
6.	I find that my mood is often influenced by how those around me are feeling.	
7.	I take on other people's stress, emotions, and/or physical symptoms.	
8.	I am often able to pick up on the subtle cues and energies that others may miss.	
9.	I find watching violent TV shows feels unbearable.	
10.	I need a long time to recuperate after being with difficult, or needy people.	
11.	When those I care about deeply are struggling, I find my focus on trying to find solutions (even if they don't ask me to).	
12.	I have a deep sense of compassion, and am driven to help those in need.	

©2022 On Purpose Transformations/Sylvia Plester-Silk. Not to be shared without written permission.

Empaths

Sylvia Plester-Silk, RSW
sylvia@OnPurposeTransformations.ca
www.OnPurposeTransformations.ca
519.822.3776

13. I have difficulty setting boundaries.	
14. I love being in nature, or with animals	
15. I find that others, even strangers, share very personal information with me.	
16. I feel other people's emotions deeply, and sometimes take them on as my own.	
17. I am affected by physical spaces. Things like clutter, colour, and placement of furniture affect my mood.	
18. I am drawn to people who are genuine and true to themselves.	
19. I often have hunches or a sense of knowing how things will turn out.	
20. I find it intolerable to learn of suffering when I can't do something about it, to the point that I feel exhausted, and overwhelmed by it.	
Total score (add up the numbers in the right-hand column)	

If you scored 20 to 45 you are an empathetic person, who copes well with many situations. Keep doing what you are doing.

If you scored 45 to 75 you have tendencies as an Empath, setting boundaries for yourself will be important to coping even better in life. You may have already learned how to cope as an empath. If not, learning about Empaths may be of benefit, so I would encourage reading or attending courses as you are called internally to do.

If you from 75 to 100 you are an Empath and are likely to find it difficult to set boundaries. You are more prone to feeling burnout and/or depression. You would benefit from learning skills and techniques to manage your energy more effectively, and to release energy that is not yours.

©2022 On Purpose Transformations/Sylvia Plester-Silk. Not to be shared without written permission.

Empathy is a great trait; however, empaths can carry the worry, concerns, and even physical pain of others, often without conscious awareness. Their energy field is so open that they can take on others' energy. Their deep compassion for others attracts pieces of other people's energy and carries it. When this happens, it feels like an exhausting burden.

How does this happen?

Imagine an empath's energy field like a huge lint filter. As they wander by others, it collects the "lint" from their energy field. These lint particles take many forms. They may be strong emotions of pain, hurt, or even joy. They might be physical ailments or even intuitive information about the person. There is no intent on the empath's part to do this; it simply happens until the empath feels exhausted and wants to isolate and be alone.

Empaths often avoid hospitals, and situations where there will be crowds. Violent movies, newscasts and TV shows can cause them to feel heavy inside and have problems sleeping, as they may take on the injuries of others portrayed through these formats.

I learned that I was an empath in my first Therapeutic Touch class in 1995. I was paired with a lovely young woman about my own age; when I sensed her energy field, I felt deep pain shoot up my arms into my shoulders, a pain so great that I immediately withdrew my hands from her energy field in alarm, feeling that I had messed something up. Calling our teacher, Evelyn, she explained that my partner had chronic pain in her shoulders. This was incredibly cool – and scary! There was little ole me believing I could never feel any form of energy, let alone something that clearly! I thought it was a cool skill and had no downside.

A few months later, on a Friday afternoon, I was taking a break at work with a couple of co-workers, and one said she had a bad toothache and would have to call the dentist for an emergency appointment. Having learned this new skill of Therapeutic Touch, I half-jokingly suggested that I could take it away using energy work. She said okay. I gave her a treatment. She immediately felt relief. I, however, had a toothache for the entire weekend —yes, in the same tooth as her. This experience was not nearly as cool!

On Monday, I called Evelyn to ask what had happened. She explained how we can take on the energy of others. She taught me to imagine wearing an energetic elastic band on my wrists when giving others energy work to prevent me from taking on their energy. Those energy bands worked as wonderful filters when I did treatments for the first several years.

I discovered that I could take on not just the physical aspects but also the emotional ones. And that I had done this my entire life: feeling the unspoken pain of my family members and carrying the burden as if it were my own. I learned the importance of managing my energy field on a daily basis. Learning to shield myself from the emotional, physical, and spiritual pain of others was a critical skill I needed.

At one point, I made a conscious decision to sense and feel the energy of others only until I had guided them through a particular issue. This worked for the most part; however, I would sometimes experience feelings of agitation and exhaustion by the end of the day with clients.

Around this time, I discovered the concept of releasing others' energy. It was powerful to be able to release the energy within a few moments and resume my day with a sense of calm freedom.

A number of years later, I realized that we can shield our energy field so that only love enters. This works to keep those energies, that are not yours to own or process, off of your energy field.

Once I learned how to be a balanced, healthy empath, I was able to use this skill to tune deeper into my clients' situations and assist them in finding hidden aspects of their lives that helped them heal.

A client I was seeing was really struggling with depression. Being concerned, I suggested they go to their doctor to have their anti-depressants reviewed. The next session they came in, they had arranged the next available doctor's appointment for the following day. We started to discuss how they were doing, and I realized that they were discussing the worries and concerns of many others. I did a quick assessment to see if they were an empath. Sure enough, they were carrying the energy of others on their energy field, which was deeply affecting their mental and physical health.

We tuned more deeply into the energy of this and released the energy that wasn't theirs. Instantly, their eyes were brighter, their posture improved, and a smile of great relief emerged.

I then taught them how to identify and release energy that was not theirs, and to shield their energy field.

If you are wondering if you are an empath, complete my Empath's Questionnaire at the beginning of this chapter.

Creating boundaries to support yourself:

- Avoid listening or watching the daily news. I stopped watching the news in 2010 and it's been incredibly helpful to me.

- Limit the amount of time that you spend with negative or needy people. This can drain you. Make decisions about who you spend your time with. Consider ending relationships that don't support you.

- Avoid watching violent TV shows and movies.

- Limit time on social media. It can be a very toxic place where many are arguing and making nasty remarks. Making active choices about where and how you spend your time is a self-care strategy—and is even more important for empaths.

Shield your energy when going out in public, and before going on social media.

Shielding Your Energy:

Bubbling:

- Ground yourself.

- Imagine a huge bubble coming from the higher realm, heaven, or the universe, depending on your personal belief system. See that bubble surround your body and energy field coming down from the top of your head into the ground by your feet.

- Breathe deeply as you do this.

Selenite Column:

(Note: Selenite is a powerful stone that helps cleanse energy. If you are unsure what it looks like, just search for a photo online.)

- Ground yourself.

- Imagine a large hollow cylinder of selenite coming from the higher realm, heaven, or the universe, depending on your personal belief system. This cylinder is the perfect size to house your energy field.

- See this cylinder gently come down around your energy field into the ground by your feet.

Releasing Foreign Energy:

When you have a strong emotion or physical sensation, you can ask your body, "Is this mine?" Listen for the slightest intuitive response from the area where you are experiencing the sensation. If yes, it belongs to you; go through the process in the chapter on Master Patterns.

If your body responds as a no, assertively state, "release this energy back to sender" with the intention that this energy goes to the higher self of the individual(s) whose energy it is. You can take a deep breath and imagine the energy being sent back to its rightful owner with loving compassion.

Alternatively, you can imagine all this energy goes into a large chamber of healing for humankind.

Chapter 8

Intuition

Intuition is the message from our inner selves and the divine. It comes in flashes of insight, having visions, and hearing important information.

Can we learn to be intuitive? Yes! However, I believe it's more about remembering we are intuitive and learning to get rid of the noise.

I believe we are all intuitive. We need to learn to live in the moment and heal past traumas and emotions so that we aren't blocked from listening to them. So, "learning" to be intuitive is about getting in touch with the stillness that lies within us.

Like anxiety, our intuition can be dismissed by mind chatter. There have been so many times that I have gotten a sense or heard a warning and ignored it, from a little whisper about taking my umbrella on a bright sunny day when no rain was forecasted, only to be caught in the rain because my mind dismissed my intuition.

I used to think that there were levels of intuition, so I was 'not really' intuitive. I thought that you were only legitimately intuitive if you saw auras and spirits and got specific messages. I didn't have these, so I discounted my abilities. I could only get little whispers or a sense of foreboding, which frankly seemed insignificant; at least, that is what my mind told me. I was wrong.

I remember many years ago searching for a new office space. I had decided it was time to upgrade the physical environment my clients entered for their sessions. The office building I was in then was not the nicest. I decided to manifest the new office by writing down everything I wanted. My list included my own bathroom, a regular cleaner, free client parking, and my desired price range.

I went to see an office, and it checked all the boxes! I was so excited to find something that was exactly what I wanted. But there was something niggling me about the landlord. He didn't make eye contact, but he told me that someone else had just called him (I didn't hear the phone ring) and was interested. In fear of losing the place (my pattern of not having enough was showing up here), I called my friend, who rushed over to give her opinion. She felt comfortable with the landlord, so I overrode my niggling feelings (aka intuition). Fast forward a few months, and I found out what all that niggling was about. The landlord and his wife had issues with me. Despite me paying my rent on time and being a great tenant, there were many challenges and conflictual interactions with them before they informed me that I could no longer speak with Richard (who was on site every day) but needed to call his wife (who was not in the office) if I needed the heat altered or anything. Then, they tried to renew my lease a month early to increase the rent. Thankfully, this allowed me to move to a better situation with no penalties, after 11 months.

Still not trusting myself and fearing making another bad decision about office space, I spoke with my business coach at the time. She shared an intuitive decision-making bypass.

Here's what to do:

Ask the universe if the option is in your highest and best interest. Ask something like this: "Please show me the following three things (pick three things that would be unusual to see at that time of year) by (the specific date you need to make the final decision)." If these three things present themselves before your date, the universe confirms that it's the right choice for you.

I picked a red canoe, Santa Claus, and a bunny. I watched Wheel of Fortune that night, and they flashed a red canoe in the background. Once again, my mind interfered—and I denied seeing it. A few days later, I was in a used furniture store, and my awareness went to the rafters, where a box with a picture of Santa was—it felt like it jumped out at me. Then, I was driving down the 401, and an entire trailer of canoes passed me in the snow. Guess what? Many of them were red! A few days later, I was walking at lunch, passed a flower shop, and glanced at the window—it was full of bunnies! I took the new office and was very happy there.

When we get information intuitively, the information we receive is often a bit surprising. It feels uplifting or inspiring, where our thoughts feel more predictable and heavier.

As we learn to follow our intuition, we will make inspired choices.

When making a decision, find the path that lights you up from inside. This is different from excitement, when our ego wants something, like the first office situation. It's a much more grounded, subtle form of excitement. There is a sense of wonder attached, and when we follow it, there is a sense of delight and magic. It's like following the breadcrumbs until we arrive at the divine solution for ourselves.

How do you tune into your intuition?

Learn to get quiet within yourself. This may require emotional healing work, meditation, and mindfulness. For me, walking in nature helps me feel grounded and present in the moment.

Practice grounding yourself on a daily basis.

Quiet your mind. It can be helpful to thank your mind and ask it to take a small break. Allow yourself to relax.

Gently focus on the individual choices you have available to you. Which one feels "most right" in your body? Do you see any energy around it? Do you hear words uttered? How does it feel in your "gut"? What do you sense about it?

Acknowledge the information you have received, even if it is vague or incomplete. Stay aware of other whispers from all your senses for the next few days. When you ask for clarity, the universe will often share more information. I find that information may come when I'm in the bathtub or when I'm not consciously "thinking" about the decision I need to make. The challenge is to pay attention to the little moments of clarity and believe them.

Keep a journal of your experiences. When you get an intuitive flash, note it (even if it's after you are caught in the rain) and what part of the information was accurate.

Note how you received the information.

- Was it a quiet whisper? What was the voice like?

- A vision? What were the qualities of it?

- A gut sensation? Where did you experience it in your body?

- A knowing? Describe what it was like.

- Did you sense it? What was that like for you?

Practice by asking yourself questions about future events and noting what you sense in your journal. Then, go back to your journal after the event and see how accurate you were. Consider partial accuracy as a valid hit. Did the accurate part of your information have a different nuance in how it got it?

Continue to pay attention and build on it!

I have learned that I am intuitive. It's a skill that I use every day in my life. Learning to trust that I can get information for myself has been incredible. I wish you the same gift; however it shows up for you is perfect!

Chapter 9

Recognizing Your Strengths

When we have experienced trauma in our younger life, we can grow up feeling that we are lacking, that we are the cause of the abuse, and otherwise, just the problem.

If we have been criticized and not supported in life, we can believe that we are not worthy, question our natural skills, and generally be incredibly hard on ourselves. We can even feel embarrassed when we receive a compliment. For some, a common pattern is to wonder what the other person might want from us in return for the kind words.

As we release the patterns that no longer serve us, we can start to see ourselves in a new light. As we have therapists, coaches, and other people in our lives who champion us, we become able to see another vision of ourselves.

Recently, a business coach told me that I don't appreciate how much I have accomplished in my life, especially given my childhood. Her statement caused me to reflect on how much I have grown and learned, and how skilled I truly am. For most of my life, I have downplayed these for fear that I was boasting and just "being too full of myself," as my mother regularly told me not to be.

It's important that we don't downplay ourselves in these ways.

It's vital that we start championing ourselves and owning our strengths and abilities as valid and valuable. It's safe to do this, and it's a powerful exercise, too!

It can be so much easier and simpler to see our faults. Then, we are more likely to experience self-critical thoughts (another pattern we can release, by the way).

It may be easier to list what you feel are your weaknesses or what you feel is wrong with you. By the way, our minds are more likely to criticize us than to see what we do well. So, we need to fight back with our goodness!

Here are a few of my recognitions about myself:

I recognize that I learned a lot as a result of my childhood abuse. As I was left as the only female in my home starting around the age of 13, for a week or two at a time, I learned how to cook meals for 6 people. I am a pretty good cook and a really great baker!

Growing up in a home with few financial resources, I am incredibly creative in finding solutions when faced with limited resources. I just have to reflect on it, and in a day or so, I often have an idea. Some of these ideas do come from my intuition—yes, and that's also a skill!

Having experienced abuse and healed from it (although I still get triggered from time to time), I am a highly skilled therapist. I am not sure I would have been as effective had I not experienced my childhood.

I am told that I am a good writer. As others shared this with me, I also learned to recognize it. And this feedback has been given to me for years, yet it was last year that I finally admitted to myself that I am a good writer.

A Note on Self-Forgiveness:

Your mind may be quite active here, and have gone into self-criticism, because none of us are perfect; we are human after all, we all make mistakes, and have things we regret about how we handled things.

You are not your mistakes. Practice self-compassion knowing that any person with the same lived experiences as you, and the same resources you had, might very likely have made the exact same choices, behaviours, and mistakes (I call these learning opportunities). We are human and we all have learning opportunities; it is up to us to gain from them and make new choices.

We can also let go of these by appreciating our humanness. Take responsibility by depatterning the underlying patterns, make amends to others as you feel is appropriate, and forgive yourself. Beating ourselves up serves no one. Forgiving ourselves allows us to move forward with grace and understanding as we make new, better choices for ourselves. As we treat ourselves with deep respect, we treat others similarly.

Now it's time to get back to owning your brilliance!

What are your special skills? Hint: These are things that come so naturally to you that you get slightly confused or irritated when others don't do it. Because they come so easily to you, you don't recognize that they are a skill, a strength you possess.

What did you gain from your trauma? This one can be hard, so simply entertain the question in your mind. See what comes to your awareness.

What do others in your life tell you is great or amazing about you? I posted a post on Facebook asking my friends to describe me in three words—that was powerful! I don't believe there was one negative trait mentioned! Give this a try (or ask people on a one-on-one basis what they appreciate about you).

Make a list. During those rough moments when you are being hard on yourself, review this list.

Celebrate yourself! You have become a victor over your circumstances. You are incredible. Do something today that honours you for being the special soul that you are.

I am confident that you have many unacknowledged gifts, talents, and skills that you deserve to acknowledge fully.

It's important to really champion ourselves so that we can shine our light more brightly.

In the words of Marianne Williamson:

"Our deepest fear is not that we are inadequate. Our deepest fear is that we are powerful beyond measure. It is our light, not our darkness that most frightens us. We ask ourselves, 'Who am I to be brilliant, gorgeous, talented, fabulous?' Actually, who are you not to be? You are a child of God. Your playing small does not serve the world. There is nothing enlightened about shrinking so that other people won't feel insecure around you. We are all meant to shine, as children do. We were born to make manifest the glory of God that is within us. It's not just in some of us; it's in everyone. And as we let our own light shine, we unconsciously give other people permission to do the same. As we are liberated from our own fear, our presence automatically liberates others."

So, go ahead and shine your light! Our world needs more light right now.

Chapter 10

Forgiveness and Letting Go

As I reflect on forgiveness, religious teachings come to mind. One must forgive and forget. It is an antiquated thought process that comes from a system of *power over* instead of *power within*.

For me, forgiveness is a kinder, gentler choice that frees you up emotionally.

When we hold onto old hurts and betrayals, waiting for someone to take responsibility and apologize, we get stuck emotionally. We slip into blame. "You did me wrong." The thought that I can only heal once you have taken responsibility fuels that blame and victim behaviour.

This is an externalized process. In doing so, we give our personal power to the very person who has harmed us. It's the opposite of acceptance, and acceptance is needed to let go.

When we are in this state and get an apology, we are still left with the unresolved original feelings. The other person may not say the exact words or acknowledge how they wounded you. Or you may hear their words as disingenuous. Then you are stuck!

When we shift the order, process these emotions fully and then make a conscious decision to release the hurt/wound, we can gain a sense of freedom and personal power. We shift into deciding our personal destiny instead of leaving it in the other person's hands.

Then, when the apology arrives, we are able to accept it or not. Either way, it no longer defines how we feel.

Years ago, an acquaintance invited me to join in a business opportunity. Months later, after a really solid friendship was developing, she became upset with me. She had asked me to sublet/share my office with a friend of hers. I agreed to speak with her friend. During the conversation, I became aware she was identifying herself as a psychologist without the credentials. I asked some questions to clarify that I wasn't making assumptions and found she only had a bachelor's degree. Due to ethical concerns, I would not sublet to her.

Within five minutes of our call ending, my business colleague called me and started to yell at me that she never wanted to speak with me again! "Do not contact me again," she emphatically stated.

I was left as part of a new organization with no one to coach me on running the business.

I stubbornly decided she would not hold me back! I reached out to others higher up in the organization explained what had happened, and asked to coach with them.

Frankly, I was pissed off with her! How dare she invite me in and abandon me without connecting me to other supports! Her behaviour was ridiculous to me—dismissive, disrespectful, and highly reactive.

Yes, I had an 'emotional charge' about this situation. To be honest, I played the victim for a while, telling my side of the story to all who would listen. I wanted to be validated, supported and coached so that I could grow.

After a while of self-righteously indulging myself in these emotions and my victimhood, I got embarrassed by my behaviour. After playing the *poor me* card by repetitively telling myself, "She did this to me," I decided I would grow more if I processed the emotions and stopped focusing on her behaviour.

I had a session with my energy therapist then, focusing on this situation. We worked through it layer by layer. I was prejudged without having my side heard or even considered. This was a common pattern throughout my life. We did a number of processes and a few sessions to get to the root cause. Beliefs like "no one listens to me," "I can't win because people judge me unfairly as mean and bad," And "I'm powerless to get ahead because I'm not likeable."

Addressing these feelings and underlying core beliefs and patterns with the assistance of my brilliant energy therapist was incredibly freeing.

I realized what had happened with this ex-business colleague was a gift. It allowed me to get even better support (including being coached by one of the most successful women in the organization). Her behaviour allowed me to work through old layers of previous traumas so that I could champion myself. Had she not acted as she had, I would not have grown in this way at that time in my life. I would have continued to see myself as broken, not worthy of being liked or listened to.

As I let this go, I decided to forgive her. Her behaviour was no longer worthy of my upset. And, holding onto these emotions and beliefs would only keep me stuck in the past. This was not where I wanted to live. I wanted so badly to grow and succeed—these old beliefs were not the road map to success.

Steps to Forgiveness:

- Get a journal or piece of paper and a pen.

- Identify the emotions that you are feeling. Embrace them. Feel them.

- What is upsetting about the current situation? What thoughts about you, your life, or how others treat you are being triggered now?

- When have these pattern(s) shown up in your life before? With whom? Write down all the instances you can think of that are related in any way.

- Notice that it was your patterns that were triggered or highlighted by this situation. Acknowledge and own this truth.

- Use the Master Release Technique from chapter 6 to work through the pattern(s) that arise.

- Can you recognize that the current situation and person come into your life to enable you to heal at a deeper level?

- Can you acknowledge that you and the other person were having a human experience to release your soul from further suffering?

- Acknowledge that you are a soul having a human experience and that you and the other person agreed at a soul level to come together in this way to enable healing and your soul's growth.

- Say, "I actively choose to free myself and (state the other person's name here) from this situation. I invite divine healing and forgiveness now."

- Take a deep breath and offer gratitude to the other person for helping you to grow.

- Thank yourself for being willing to heal, let the situation go, and release your hurt.

I invite you to do this healing exercise about situations that are holding you back today.

You deserve to experience emotional freedom!

Kind People

It is in the times when I reflect on safety, both emotional and physical, that I sincerely appreciate those kind, caring folks who entered my life. Sometimes, for moments, days, and/or years, for they were the ones who acknowledged me as valid, special, and important.

While they seemed like rare gems in my mind, I am aware that my bowl of sacred, beautiful gems is overflowing. Why is it in the dark moments that all I saw was the lack?

It was a poignant contrast between love and criticism. My child self felt unworthy of anything but criticism. The habit in our home of being sarcastic in a hurtful cutting way cut deeply into my ego. As a result, my sense of self, my diminished self-worth, was like a heap of scrap —seemingly with little value.

Yet, these angelic gems, these people, showed me a different reflection of my inner perfection and value. I hesitated to own it, fearing what would follow, often the criticism or belittling. Yet it was not of these people's capacity—but a gift for me directly from the divine.

My first memory of this was when my siblings left me on the cement steps of the church for my vacation bible school so they wouldn't be late for their classes at a different church. I tried the door, finding it locked, and thought I would be left alone all day. I was frightened and started to cry. Along came the reverend's wife, who gently placed her arm around frightened 5-year-old-me in comfort. I was crying, thinking I had been left forever, and she had clear, beautiful eyes and expressions of pure love and caring. The comfort from a stranger, the people my family taught me to fear and mistrust. Was I bad trusting her?

I have had many experiences of kindness in my life. The expression my soul had craved and that my mind questioned. The comfort within my heart and body wanted to override the doubt. Yet the fear instilled in me was hard to reject.

My friend Nancy's family was another gift in my life. I went to their home on weekends, where it was relaxed. I remember playing, laughing and having fun. I was so fortunate they invited me to join them on vacation when I was around 10 or 12. I got to travel across beautiful Canada, feeling wanted. I will always be grateful for their role in my life. They taught me about volunteering and caring for others.

Another gift came years later, after working with Trish, the energetic therapist whose eyes of love shone intensely into the recesses of my being, illuminating the love and light in my being. She taught me my true self-worth and the love that I could now show myself, and permitted me to break away from the hurtful darkness of family to the sunlight of possibility and love. She taught me that I was valid. She astounded me by responding to my needs, not requiring deep reasons, and honouring me fully.

While we may not have grown up in the most loving homes, we all have human angels that see something special in us. Our patterns will often deny this, but fortunately we can release these outdated patterns.

These lovely beings help to insulate us from trauma. Learning to accept these loving views can take some work. It is well worth reflecting on what they see in us.

Pull out your journal and make a list of those people who did this for you. Include tiny moments when you remember being cared for, as they are a reflection of you.

Feel the love that has been shown to you without any expectations in return.

This is a vibrant love, that you truly deserve! Own it and allow that love and acceptance energy fully into your mind, body and spirit.

With love,
Sylvia

About the Author

Sylvia Plester-Silk, RSW, is an award-winning intuitive Social Worker who integrates traditional therapy with energy work and Akashic Readings to help individuals transform their lives into ones that are fully on purpose.

In 1988, way back in ancient history as she likes to say, Sylvia graduated from the Social Work program at Ryerson Polytechnical Institute (now Toronto Metropolitan University). Over the next 2 decades, while working for multiple community agencies, she guided thousands of individuals through addictions, mental health, and trauma to find their way. While she was powerful in this work, her results became exponential when she added energy therapies into her practice in the mid-1990s.

In 2004, Sylvia opened her private practice. Her clients find her direct, honest approach refreshing. *On Purpose Transformations* guides her clients in achieving emotional freedom, harmonious relationships, and a joy-filled life.

Sylvia is the author of *Unleashing Team Potential: Lessons for Managers from My Canine Friends,* which was highlighted in the Globe and Mail.

She is a regular guest on podcasts where she inspires audiences with her insights. She is also a seasoned speaker and workshop facilitator. Contact her at sylvia@onpurposetransformations.ca for booking information.

Sylvia finds herself energized by nature, whether at the local beaches of Georgian Bay or the majestic tip of Machu Picchu.

She lives in Guelph, Ontario, Canada with her husband and her dog Josee.

Sylvia invites you to learn more at her website www.OnPurposeTransformations.ca.

www.ingramcontent.com/pod-product-compliance
Lightning Source LLC
LaVergne TN
LVHW051659080426
835511LV00017B/2637